RECESSION MARKETING

JOSEPH FINORA

ASJA PRESS
NEW YORK   BLOOMINGTON

Recession Marketing

ASJA Press
an imprint of iUniverse, Inc.

iUniverse books may be ordered through booksellers or by contacting:

iUniverse
1663 Liberty Drive
Bloomington, IN 47403
www.iuniverse.com
1-800-Authors (1-800-288-4677)

Because of the dynamic nature of the Internet, any Web addresses or links contained in this book may have changed since publication and may no longer be valid.

ISBN: 978-1-4401-4994-8 (sc)

Printed in the United States of America

iUniverse rev. date: 7/7/2009

For further information, additional copies or a

no-obligation consultation, contact Joseph Finora at: jfinora@optonline.net.

All calls, consultations and client information are kept confidential.

To the four who matter to me most: Mary Grace, Joseph, James and Gabrielle

CONTENTS

INTRODUCTION
MARKET YOUR WAY OUT OF THIS RECESSION

Are you working on your marketing stimulus plan? Innovative marketing strategies are needed to thrive in any downturn and during this recession ideas are plentiful.

Getting from nowhere to somewhere however, requires a roadmap and there are many points to consider. There are countless stories about how tough it is to market during recessions, but there are always specific frugal and effective marketing tools one can use to increase their return on investment.

With a tough climate on the horizon, there are still a few items no forward-looking marketing plan should be without but during an economic downtown other factors should also be given prime consideration. Your recession marketing plan should contain frugal, ethical and effective strategies that can immediately boost marketing return on investment.

To keep business percolating, we must emphasize previous successes to hold on to our best clients. This is a time for relationship building and giving your clients the best service and attention possible. Differentiate yourself from competitors and emphasize the benefits you can bring to your clients. Keeping a stable of buyers during this financial maelstrom will pay off in the coming years where tremendous growth can take place.

In today's economic climate the first thing that comes to mind is price, but it's not so easy to undercut the next guy when your goal is to provide long-term value and service to build a lasting customer relationship. It's more about what additional features and benefits a you can offer, that is what will drive traffic and sales and help differentiate you from your competitors. You already have a captive audience with your existing clientele. But how do you keep clients from going elsewhere in such a competitive environment?

Price erosion generally runs rampant in a recession and many businesses will operate at a loss simply to maintain relationships with existing clients and keep their machines running. The market is changing. The market is always changing. Change is the one aspect we expect to continue. Your business probably needs to change with the times but you must also keep an eye on the bottom line.

Other things each of us should understand are how new approaches in digital and social media marketing can launch your company into new market opportunities. Not yet as technologically savvy when it comes to marketing as you'd like to be? Make a point to change that ASAP as Internet marketing is one of the bright spots on the landscape. A good first and easy step is to check out the Search Engine Marketing Professional Organization (**www.sempo.org**). The mission of this global, non-profit organization is to serve the search-engine marketing industry and the marketing professionals engaged in it. Its purpose is to provide a foundation for industry growth through building stronger relationships, fostering awareness, providing education, promoting the industry, generating research, and creating a better understanding of search and its role in marketing.

Making technology play a larger role in your marketing efforts can help your business better adapt in today's unpredictable economy. Other items that should be high on the agenda should be a willingness to adjust prices and promotions without sacrificing market share, quality or your brand image. Also keep a sharp eye on accountability and obtaining measurable results from your investments while improving strategic and tactical planning with marketing techniques and tools.

The shrinking economy, no doubt, will affect each of us in the years ahead as businesses across all verticals may cut budgets and staff. Each of us needs to embrace new technologies and communication strategies. We can also use the web to measure the success and failures of campaigns through the use of technologies such as personalized URLs. Yet while Internet technologies are high in the area of interest we must use traditional techniques to enhance existing web efforts and not compete against them.

Similarly, it is important for each of us to think of ourselves as the customer and consult with clients on ways to provide the best response for every dollar spent. Long-term client-vendor relationships are the cornerstone of every successful business.

Growing and/or preserving business during a recession is challenging but not impossible. All recessions are temporary. The sooner we work to get out from one the sooner stronger businesses will emerge.

CHAPTER 1

WHAT'S ALL THE 'BUZZ' ABOUT 'NEW MEDIA'?

USING THE INTERNET TO YOUR ADVANTAGE

Many of the more traditional marketers can lately often be heard complaining that "things just aren't like they used to be." They couldn't be more right.

The Internet, many of them charge, is taking away sales and eroding profits. But have you considered learning how to work with the many forms of this new media to stage a counter-attack and reposition your business on a sign of marketing strength?

Marketing is a dynamic phenomenon with changes taking place all the time. Cutting-edge marketers can now leverage their business at a faster speed than previous generations by harnessing the power of "new media." Going beyond basic e-mail marketing, social media sites like Facebook, Twitter and LinkedIn are being used to spread the word about oneself more effectively and with a wider range than anything that's come before. And while this is considered a "young person's" medium, there's no reason others cannot utilize these tools. Other good business networking sites include: TalkBizNow and Spoke.

Learning to communicate on the social-web environment means reaching others in a new medium. You do not need to completely re-learn everything you knew about marketing. It does mean they have to open their mind to new possibilities, social change and rethinking past practices.

Consider that Facebook is home to a good demographic group – educated 18-26 year-olds. While this is for a generation that's grown up in front of a computer, social networking is not about making direct sales but rather about building a presence and reputation that associates you with your business and the solutions you provide. But beware, such sites can be brutally honest as people tend to speak freely on them. What this means for you is that you need to be prepared to deliver as promised and back up everything you say about yourself and your company.

IT'S FAST

One of the key benefits however, is that social marketing/networking can provide an increased Return-on-Investment (ROI) as well as a positive change in your business image. It's also very cost-efficient and low risk when compared with other forms of traditional marketing. Another benefit is that with this type of marketing you can learn a great deal about your client/prospect base whether you make a sale or not and begin to compile potentially useful information while spreading your business reputation.

Consider LinkedIn the leading business-networking site. It boasts some 35 million registered users and is technically a general social-networking website but is mainly used for business purposes. Facebook dwarfs all competitors with some 235 million users around the world but most are on for social purposes. Other general social-networking sites include Classmates. com and Tagged.com. Others get specific such as BlackPlanet which is for African-Americans. CafeMom serves mothers. Care2 is for green living and social activism.

Facebook, the giant of the space, is predominantly a social site but it is occasionally used for business purposes by participants. Groups founded online tend to operate in a faster dynamic than their more traditional counterparts such as Chamber of Commerce or Rotary Groups. Facebook is great for keeping yourself in front of those who you wish to stay in touch with. It's faster than traditional means of communication as you can learn so much more about a person or promote information about yourself and have it read much more quickly than a traditional way.

Facebook can give you a fast start which can be critical when you want others to know things about you and your business as social networking builds a kind of excitement and grows interest. With social-networking sites, when one posts information on their profile, "friends" those who've asked to correspond with you and your network, automatically receive it, providing extraordinary marketing reach with minimal cost and effort. Face-to-face marketing is never going to go away but with social networking, things will move at an accelerated pace.

Anyone can get started on Facebook and ask to open a dialogue with others who are interested in learning more about his business. Do not view it as a means for direct sales but as a way to cost effectively grow your reputation and to learn about what prospects are thinking. With some 235 million users there are bound to be a few interested in what you offer. It can be an ideal way to lead others to your company's website and to build up an "exclusive" list of prospects who you may wish to invite to a virtual tour of your office or open an online dialogue and cultivate clients you'd most likely never contact were it not for the ability to reach out through the world wide web.

How's that for fighting back against the Internet?

CHAPTER 2
BREAKING THROUGH BARRIERS TO 'YES'

AND WHY PRICE CAN BE IRRELEVANT

Successfully marketing your company can sometimes be described as an ongoing lesson in breaking through barriers. Sometimes telling someone you can do it better, faster or cheaper is not enough. There's the matter of getting a key decision-maker to answer your phone call or make that vital initial introduction. And then there's the all important follow-up. Further complicating the communication process are issues like scheduling, time budgeting and sometimes the all-imposing secretary or "executive assistant" who's more of a screen than an administrative aide as their main responsibility is to selectively weed out the mail or methodically dispose of the telephone messages – making it virtually impossible for new vendors to penetrate and reach the desired decision-maker. What's a hardworking marketer to do?

A lot of sales success can be traced to paying attention to the details. Promptly returning phone calls and being on time for appointments give the impression that you're serious. Picking up new clients is hard work but it's just as essential to keep your present clients. It's more effective when you're working for the long term. This is how to build a business.

And a job well done can lead to referrals. People in every industry change jobs and share information. A stellar track record can win you a key referral and lead to a new business stream. But no one can wait for someone to start talking about them, so it can pay to ask. It's no one else's responsibility to grow your business.

You can "create" referrals with a simple and honest approach. Saying something over lunch to a good customer like: "I'm trying to grow my business and would appreciate any leads you can provide." Or: "Since you're happy with our service would you know anyone else who we might be able to help?" If they provide you with a name or two, quickly get in touch with the prospect and if you're forced to leave a message be sure to mention who referred you. If you're using e-mail for the follow-up, don't be shy about adding that person to the "cc" list." This adds to your integrity and shows you're confident and serious about speaking with the prospect.

But in these types of communications, don't be clever, cute or overly friendly. Remember, this is new business you're trying to cultivate. Prospects want to know who you are, what you're offering and how they can benefit before they start to give you business, generally before you meet with them in person. It can be challenging but remaining on topic and delivering a brief but factual message like the following is usually a good basic strategy:

Mr. Jones, Sam Sample of XYZ Marketing suggested I contact you re: our services. We've been providing Sam's company with first-rate color service on time and on budget for five years. If you have a few moments in the near future, I'd like to show what we can do for your company and have mailed a few samples to your office for review. Thank you for your consideration. I hope we can meet soon.

Once you've sent the e-mail and samples, be prepared to follow-up. Lot's of business is lost by those who make a strong presentation but fail to continue the relationship. A vendor who follows-up is demonstrating that they're serious about the prospect's business. This helps form an impression on the prospect that you'll do a good job.

Every bit of client communication you have boils down to marketing. None of your communications should have empty phrases like "Our service is absolutely peerless" or "We go the extra mile for you." Professionals are looking for other professionally minded business people. What they are looking for is a vendor who's going to help solve their problems and meet their business goals. Your communication should contain keywords and factual concepts noting the following:

- Your Expertise: Why should someone come to you?
- Your Key Personnel: How much experience does the person actually handling my job have?
- Technical Capabilities: Is your equipment cutting-edge?
- Customer Service: Are calls promptly returned?
- Client-Retention Ratio: Do clients remain with you?
- Reliability: Do you meet deadlines and budgets?
- Extras: What's different about your firm? What's your strongest asset?

PRICE CAN BE IRRELEVANT

Price is not on the list above because the prospect who shops strictly on the basis of price usually will not be a good, long-term client. While prices need to be competitive, a client whose key concern is getting the lowest price possible is usually not going to be around for a very long time and probably will not be a "quality customer." Once someone else undercuts you they're gone, no matter how good a job you've done. Marketing plans need to account for this.

Regularly being in touch with clients and prospects helps contribute to your business reputation. If you want to be a candidate for future work, you need to be always available and accessible. Promptly return phone calls and e-mails. Thoroughly answer prospects' questions and if it will help, have them speak with the right person at your plant if the question is of a technical nature. Things like these help build integrity and show client commitment. And when done consistently, they'll get you an audience with that elusive decision-maker.

CHAPTER 3
IS YOUR OFFICE CRISIS-READY?

WHY THE TIME TO DRAFT YOUR CRISIS PLAN IS NOW

Crisis and disaster planning are now common business-operation terms. Almost every business could be consumed by a nearly endless variety of crises, from a natural disaster such as a flood or hurricane which can devastate a facility to a terrorist strike to a deranged employee or customer bent on revenge to financial turmoil. Anything hurting your business, its reputation or ability to grow sales, collect revenue or move forward in any way can be a form of crisis.

According to a PricewaterhouseCoopers 2007 survey, 49% of all US-based multinationals have experienced a high-level crisis in the last three years – some event that had a catastrophic impact on one or more business units. Some 53% of these companies said they had experienced a true crisis due to a natural disaster, while 31% reported a complete shutdown of a business unit while 20% reported significant problems due to management upheaval.

While it's of course impossible to predict when a crisis may strike, it's very reasonable to prepare for one and there are certain steps every business should take in order to be ready should one of your worst fears materialize.

COMMUNICATION, THE FIRST STEP

A business-continuity plan prepares your operation for a wide range of events that could interrupt your business as opposed to simply doing damage. Though a storm may not structurally damage your facility it may cut off power for an extended time period -- possibly days, adversely affecting equipment and operations. It may make it impossible for key employees to get to work. A key customer suddenly declaring bankruptcy may force you to absorb a staggering financial loss. What steps would you take under these circumstances? Do you have back-up equipment? An alternative location? An available line of credit?

It's easy to lose sight of the fact that communication runs two ways. The more you invest in communicating with key staff, suppliers and customers, the more likely they will be able to give you potentially valuable news and feedback. Some of the best ideas trickle up the chain -- if you're not listening you will not be able to benefit. Primary and secondary communication representatives should be named and staff should be given their home telephone, cell phone and e-mail addresses. Be sure this is updated and circulated to new personnel. Not informing employees can lead to such ramifications as the wrong message being communicated. Frontline staff, such as call center representatives, company officers and anyone who directly deals with vendors, clients and other business partners need to be consistently informed of what's taking place within their company should a business-crippling disaster strike.

Overlooking the effects of not communicating with staff can add a second level to the crisis you're trying to manage. By regularly communicating with staff when they first join your company, management is setting a good policy so that should a crisis strike, everyone will know where to turn.

WHO'S ON FIRST?

During normal conditions but especially during a crisis, staff should be the first to know about key issues before news is released. It's demoralizing when employees learn about events at their job site from a news report or neighbor. It also erodes trust staff has in management.

Keeping control of all the moving parts is one of the keys to crisis-communication management. Too often management focuses on the technical systems that need to be replicated. While it's very important to get your office up and running as soon as possible, in the event of a disaster that makes using a physical location not available, the initial communications to staff, clients and the public can have a dramatic effect on the lasting results of a crisis. Your image and reputation may be at stake. How you make sure all personnel are informed and react in times of crises happens with proper planning. Every business should have a detailed "decision" tree of who is to be contacted, what should be communicated and when.

WHAT ABOUT INSURANCE?

It's a common and shortsighted mistake to think one's insurance policy will cover disaster-related losses. While an insurance policy may cover you for a material loss it cannot prevent damage to your professional reputation. What if a partner's involved in a scandal? He can be dismissed but how will your reputation recover? Cutting-edge firms aim to minimize such risks with long-range, comprehensive planning.

What about an employee who charges unfair dismissal or harassment or a severe workplace injury or accident? How would you handle the customer who sues or refuses to pay because a job "did not meet his standards," or publicly argues he was "misled" by a representative of your firm? Scenarios such as these can become disastrous as well as distracting and possibly result in a huge public relations problem for your firm, in addition to any financial hardship it may cause.

Umbrella policies are used to provide extra protection and can be especially helpful in the case of claims exceeding the limits of one's general liability insurance. In today's legal climate, as claims grow in size and number along with settlements, the need for umbrella coverage is also increasing, supplementing basic liability and protecting clients from unforeseen coverage gaps. While they frequently carry a relatively high deductible, consider that if you're required to pay $1 million in a judgment – not an unusual amount by today's standards – but have only $500,000 in liability coverage, the umbrella policy would supply the remaining $500,000. Umbrella coverage usually does not start until other insurance coverage limits are exhausted. Defending even a frivolous or groundless lawsuit can be expensive and without such coverage such a scenario as described above can easily cripple a business's future income as it struggles to make settlement payments over time. And although business people tend to purchase inadequate amounts of coverage no one wants to learn too late that they have coverage gaps. Fortunately an umbrella policy can be, especially versus the costs of judgments, very reasonable thus protecting your company with more in-depth coverage in the case of an exorbitant claim or claims.

While umbrella coverage can turn out to be a business's best friend, those considering such coverage should purchase it from the same company that's providing their general liability policy. The reason is that in addition to a premium discount, the possible headache of dealing with several insurance companies in the case of a claim would be eliminated as there's the risk of each provider attempting to shift payment responsibility to the other, resulting in further frustration for you.

GETTING STARTED

It's very common for a company to spend significant resources on the creation of a crisis plan only to find out too late that it is either incomplete or out of date. Be ready to commit the required resources and mind share of senior management to establish a long-term plan and periodically review and update it. The time to form a plan if you have none is now. Get staff involved right away. Make sure everyone knows their role and where to turn. If your plan is in a thick binder collecting dust in a drawer, now is the time to reevaluate it and make it part of your active-management process. Any crisis-communication planning is only as good as its last test.

A Crisis-Communications Blueprint

- Be sure staff knows who the primary and secondary communication personnel are and how to reach them.
- Keep staff's home and cell phones as well as personal e-mail addresses updated.
- Be sure a media-relations representative is appointed and accessible.
- Have a decision-tree circulated with contact numbers. Regularly update it.
- Be sure staff knows where any emergency location is and how to get there.
- Be sure staff understands privacy issues.
- Create and distribute an office-communications policy including a section on how to stay in touch during an emergency and how to handle client and media calls.
- Have adequate back-up office space (emergency location) which can house key personnel as well as necessary equipment.

CHAPTER 4
HARNESSING THE CULT OF YOUR PERSONALITY

DON'T LOSE YOUR EGO, USE IT

Is the egomaniac down the hall in the office filled with plaques, awards and photos of his boat and Aspen vacations getting on your nerves? Before leveling the criticism, examine the evidence. Is he broadcasting a false status or are his accounts truly increasing each year? Is he regularly cultivating centers of influence or exploring new marketing avenues? Is he consistently providing innovative solutions for clients -- doing the types of things that get people talking and reaping the rewards? If so, this may be a case of an ego as a result of successful behavior.

It's often said, "If you don't use it, you lose it." The rule may also apply to ego. Psychologically speaking, ego is the force that drives us. It's the psychological phenomenon that enables each of us to pursue our aspirations – whether they be getting the football across the goal line or nailing that monster account. According to psychology pioneer Sigmund Freud, the ego is the key component of our psyches, empowering us to manage day-to-day realities.

In the everyday lexicon however, ego has come to be more closely associated with attitude. Do perennial top sales representatives have super-size egos or do they just appear that way? It's hard to imagine a leading sales rep being overly humble or withdrawn.

While they may outwardly flaunt their success among peers at the annual sales conference or around the office, when it comes to client contact are they actually capable of managing their ego or better yet, controlling it and using it to their advantage. As it's absolutely vital to have confidence in this business no one should let their ego run out of control to the point where their head won't fit through the door. Why? Clients want to see confidence. If you're not completely knowledgeable and comfortable with your recommendations they'll sense this and you'll pay for it.

But if a certain ego level can be healthy and productive how can one keep it at the right level? There's a big difference between confidence and cockiness. The former drives sales, the latter drives clients away. Sounds obvious but it can be easily overlooked.

Nearly everyone feels at one time like they've made a thousand cold calls only to receive an equal number of rejections. It's easy to see how one's ego can take a beating. It's not as easy to see why those who survive in this business not only bounce back from rejection but grow from it.

Consider rejection as an opportunity to analyze client behavior, learn more and turn a negative into a positive. While your ego shows confidence you cannot let it get in the way of the client who has to come first. Ask about the client's needs, present a sensible plan and explain the reasoning behind your recommendations. Giving the client what he needs is the true royal treatment.

When a sudden rejection derails what looked like a promising sale, that's when you should be maintaining focus and communication. Sincerely ask the prospect what went wrong. Do not be confrontational. There could be something you were not aware of, like a sudden change in the company which can be serious or something frivolous like a relative who just got into the business. Ask if you could meet again in the near future. They'll usually agree. Rationally explain your recommendations and qualifications. Don't take it personally and don't let your ego get in the way.

Marketing yourself can sometimes be described as an ongoing lesson in breaking through barriers, which is the determined person's way of handling what can seem like a constant stream of rejection. Sometimes telling someone you can do it better, faster or cheaper is not enough. There's the matter of getting a key decision-maker to answer your phone call or make that vital introduction. There's the preparation and follow-up and the all important process of winning the client's trust. Further complicating the communications procedure are issues like scheduling or the all-imposing partner who's more of a barrier to keep you from moving forward. Hurdles like these can weaken the most durable egos. How does one circumvent the barriers and get the client to "yes" while putting his often bruised ego to work in the process?

A strong and healthy ego is indicative of someone secure in who he is and confident in his ability to communicate and be believed. A sales representative with an overpowering ego is demonstrating basic insecurity -- a sign of weakness. While ego is the desire for achievement and significance, maturity, integrity and character are essential to keep egos in check.

No matter what the size of one's ego, at the end of the day it's the client who's the boss. Therefore, it's vital to remember the things they want which is usually service. No one likes to think they've been forgotten. What may appear to be little things are often actually important.

It's unforgivable not to return client phone calls or be late for appointments. These give the perception that not only is the client not important in your eyes but that you're more important than he is. That's a case of an ego run amuck which will backfire.

But egos are not one-size-fits-all products. Like a person's sense of humor, they're unique. What may come across as a misanthropic ego for one may be interpreted as confidence by another. Various clients will also perceive and react differently to your behavior. The same attitude that creates a happy, productive relationship for Client A may not translate well for Clients B or C – here lies a new angle for the cult of one's personality which is inseparable from a sales or management style.

By checking one's egos at the door one becomes a doormat. Try empathizing. If a client complains about the challenges of taking care of new personnel point out solutions that may help -- meet the prospect/client at the same level. If she has a firm handshake, speaks in short declarative sentences and carries herself with poise then do the same.

Similarly, others feel ego, an offshoot of emotion, can be mutually felt among likeminded individuals and you may wish to move to capitalize on this phenomenon. Believe in yourself and what you offer and prospects will generally respond accordingly.

The winning businessperson should rely on knowledge and skill and realize that the good prospects and clients are often smart and somewhat skeptical. Empathize with them while communicating your expertise. Putting the prospect's best interest first almost always wins. A confident person shouldn't need to check their ego at the door providing they remember that the client always comes first. Once they master this and their business flourishes, some ego can be warranted.

CHAPTER 5
THE GREATEST RISK OF ALL – NOTHING

YOU HAVE NOTHING TO FEAR EXCEPT NOTHING ITSELF

This is not a take-off of the Seinfeld episode regarding a show about "nothing." It's about actually doing nothing. Doing nothing to grow your business. Being content with the status quo. Expecting everything to remain the same.

For starters, consider that there is no such thing as the "status quo." For thousands of years, from the days of Confucius, philosophers have been teaching that change is inevitable and we must prepare for and embrace it if we are to succeed. To paraphrase the "history" adage: Those who don't prepare for change surely will perish from it. But how can one prepare for change, which in many cases is unpredictable.

The truth is, life changes on a daily basis – maybe in a subtle way, maybe dramatically or somewhere in between but each day is different from the one that preceded it and will also differ from the one that follows. How you react to these subtle and not-so-subtle changes may spell the difference between business success and failure.

Look at your customer base. People move. They change jobs. Leave the state. Companies come and go. Technology marches forward. Factors like consolidation make competition tighter. On the other hand, emerging technologies present new business opportunities. To grow you can't remain behind the curve, you've got to learn how to read the curve, figure where it's going and then hit it out of the park.

The same is true for your business.

But what about the other business persona? Here I'm talking about the person who's constantly saying, to lean on James Bond: The world is not enough. The one's who want each day to be bigger, faster and more productive than any of its predecessors. There is a dose of unreality in this philosophy as well but if a sales manager had to choose one over the other, surely she'd select the hard-charging, high-flyer rather than anyone content with keeping things the way they are. Here are some key questions to ask when trying to cultivate the champion many feel lies within each of us:

1. Do you have nearly everything you want or are you harboring feelings of discontent or dissatisfaction?
2. Do you embrace technology and/or other changes in your life or do you wish things were like they were during the "good old days"?
3. Do you feel greater fulfillment can be found with a more productive business life?
4. Are you trying to work smarter, harder or both?
5. Are you regularly trying to figure better ways to do/grow business?
6. Do you consider partnerships/relationships that can enhance your business?
7. Are you committed to providing your clients with the highest service level possible?
8. Is your office organized to provide maximum efficiency?
9. Are you satisfied with what you do and your performance/quality level?
10. Do you have a life outside of business?

How you answer these questions may determine if you're on the road to greater production or will remain mired in the status quo. A lot of it is focused on the intangibles inside the person rather than outside factors. "Do you have a relentless burning desire to succeed? Can you cultivate and then unleash a mindset that can help you develop the attitude of a high achiever?

Stuck in a sales and marketing rut? You're probably a business wizard but can you truly prospect? We each know about cold calling and mass mailing but is that all there is? Will these techniques make you a stand-out professional? Probably not. Most prospects, will agree they've reached the saturation point when it comes to these methods. But if you creatively prospect, chances are that in the client's mind you'll get their attention and place yourself ahead of the competition from the opening bell. An ongoing mantra of your day-to-day marketing should be to regularly stimulate highly qualified new clients while servicing and presenting existing ones with new ideas and pointing out ways you can help them. It's this type of networking that generally leads to referrals – which typically have a very strong "close" ratio as informed clients make the best clients.

Every business is in a constant state of change. A direct mail package that generated a boatload of inquiries a few years ago may not resonate with today's prospects. The explosion of personal media, desk-top technology, mergers and acquisitions and the drive towards greater outsourcing has created a more savvy client but these changes also bring opportunity to those who can spot and act on them because shifting consumer demand and preferences spur industry evolution. Consumers have a greater ability to shop and build unbiased knowledge. Plus an increase in assortment of products and services gives them greater choice. However, those who understand these phenomena can often benefit from them.

By presenting yourself as a creative marketer, you're also viewed as a clever problem-solver – one who truly thinks out of the box. And as business becomes increasingly competitive, someone who's able to embrace change and offer cutting-edge solutions can be a valuable commodity. No matter what you're specialty the market is wide open for avant-garde marketers.

There are numerous challenges when it comes to providing first-class marketing and other support services but the payoff is that determination to build a better business will help you grow while providing client confidence in the company behind you. In the long run, this should make all the difference by helping to strengthen relationships and business. Throughout it all, remember that change is inevitable, the status quo does not exist and that doing nothing is the greatest risk of all.

CHAPTER 6

HOW TO MEET THE PRESS OR 'I WANT MY CNBC!'

DEVELOPING A MEDIA-RELATIONS STRATEGY CAN HELP TELL THE WORLD WHAT YOUR BUSINESS IS ALL ABOUT

No businessperson should be asking: Why do I need to develop a media-relations strategy?

Instead, they should be asking: When will I launch my media-relations strategy?

In many ways, it's never been easier to get one's name in the paper. There is a plethora of websites, talk shows and publications – each looking for expert sources. Similarly, it's never been trickier to find the right outlet, avoid traps and say what will position you as an authority to help grow your business.

Getting on TV sounds simple – call the station. Tell them how knowledgeable you are and wait for Brian Williams to call. Like the prospect who says he'll do just fine on his own, those serious about getting in print usually see the best results when going with a professional.

SELECTING A REP

Before interviewing media-relations pros, decide what is your primary objective? While it's exciting to see your name in print, it's important to think beyond that. How do you want your practice to be portrayed? What contributions can a comprehensive media-relations strategy make towards helping you achieve your goals?

When interviewing media-relations firms consider that a relatively small company could be well served by a firm of about the same size. Check credentials. Ask for references. Be sure they're familiar with your industry but not working for a competitor. Ask to see samples of their work and of the "placements" they've obtained. Tell them as much as you can about your business. What your goals are and why you think media relations can help. Make sure you're comfortable with the person who will be working on your account, as well as the fees and schedule. If you're not prepared to jump into an ongoing arrangement ask about "project work." Many firms will start new accounts this way and decide later whether a long-term strategy should be pursued. At that point the firm would be put on retainer by your office and you'd pay a monthly fee depending on services.

While no one can make guarantees, your media-relations rep should feel confident about being able to get you reasonable coverage in the outlets you desire. They should also be ready to write and distribute press releases, prepare a media/information kit, organize a press event and when the time comes, coach you on dealing with reporters. Writing and distributing a press release one time shouldn't be more than a couple of hundred dollars for a local firm. Be sure that "reasonable re-writes" are included or whether you'll be charged every time the writer sits down at his desktop. Ask if they'll provide telephone follow-up after each release. After about three months you should know whether the relationship will be effective.

While often mentioned in the same conversation, media relations is not the same as advertising. Although both can be effective the difference boils down to one of credibility. An advertisement is a paid-for message. The buyer controls everything about it. When a reporter calls for your opinion, she's doing so because she believes you're a subject-area expert. When she signs her name on the article, it's a subtle yet strong endorsement of your expertise.

OFFER YOURSELF AS AN EXPERT

Local newspapers and radio stations are often the easiest places to start. This will give you exposure as an authority in your area of expertise and at the same time, put your name in front of prospects in your business region. Being seen as an expert is different from being a publicity hound. One smart way to avoid being typecast as a blatant publicity seeker and present yourself as an expert is to stick with what you know. This is known as "positioning."

If you're a manufacturing expert and a writer asks you some questions on technology the best answer may be something like this: *Sorry, I generally don't get involved with technology issues and therefore, would probably not be your best source. I can recommend, however, that you speak with Jennifer Jones. She's a great technology consultant. Here's her number. Please keep me in mind for any manufacturing questions you may have. May I send you a few story ideas?*

Better to turn it down then provide a poor answer and risk embarrassing yourself and annoying the reporter. With the response above, chances are the reporter appreciated the candor, the qualified contact and the opportunity for more story ideas.

Consider this: say you've recently installed a new, state-of-the-art, inventory-management platform in your office. That's news. Make a list of the platform's capabilities. Maybe it will result in the creation of new jobs or open new markets for you – these events can be news.

Or maybe a member of your firm recently received a new industry designation. Examples such as these are hard news which generally finds a home in local media outlets. The next step would be to locate which newspapers in your area have lively business sections. Don't know? Ask your friends and neighbors what they read. What radio and cable television programs do they listen to?

It's generally advisable to avoid "give-away" or free newspapers – the kind you find on your doorstep on Saturday mornings. While they have some readership, you'll usually get far more mileage out of a mention in a paper with a paid circulation rather than the local (and free) shopper. The reason? People read and trust the papers they purchase. Free newspapers are discarded at a much higher frequency rate than are those that people purchase and they are largely read by those seeking something for free. Other outlets may be newsletters or web sites that reach the groups you're hoping to target. These should be on your media "hit list."

A supplier or other firms with whom you do business may be able to help you get in touch with the media. This person may be listed as Corporate Communications Representative. Find out who that person is and let him or her know your goals. Ask that he take your contact information and pass it on to a reporter when the right opportunity presents itself. Or they may direct you to an outside firm or freelancer who specializes in your area.

Like long-term business planning, while there are risks involved and it's generally unwise to make promises, a good media-relations plan usually works best when engineered for the long term and with the help of a professional.

Still not convinced on the power of media relations? Listen to what one New York-based businessperson says. "If reporters are not calling you, then they're calling someone else. I'd rather see my name in the paper than my competitor's."

Note: For further reading we recommend: *Media Relations and Creative Marketing Tips by Joseph Finora.*

CHAPTER 7
THE MESSAGE IS IN THE E-MAIL

GETTING STARTED IN E-MARKETING

Like nearly everything in this industry, marketing has evolved and continues to do so. E-marketing, or using electronic means, usually e-mail and Internet Search Optimization (ESO) to promote your company is moving with increasing speed to the forefront and here's why. E-marketing can be relatively inexpensive once staff is trained on the appropriate software, which usually must be purchased. It's fast, practically instantaneous. It's cutting-edge, meaning it helps elevate your image to a firm that does more than offer traditional printing services. The impression it makes is that a firm that's aligned itself with an e-marketing campaign is probably very technologically savvy. And increasingly, clients are expecting it.

E-marketing proves to be a necessary tool for customer retention and increased Return-on-Investment (ROI) in the current market notes eMarketer, (www.emarketer.com) a business research and consulting firm which adds that e-mail marketing ranks number-one for customer retention and delivers the highest (ROI) of any marketing method.

With many businesses reporting slowing sales and the cost of attracting new customers climbing, e-marketing to one's existing customer base can be a sound and low-cost investment. A Jupiter Research (www.jupiterresearch.com)study found that targeted e-mail marketing campaigns can generate nine times more revenue than mailings.

The main benefit is more business from existing clients and new business from new ones and possibly an increase in the positive perception of the company. Clients and prospects see that you're doing something different and innovative. Business owners and managers want to work with innovative and tech-savvy people. Such marketing campaign can lead to more meetings with prospects, past clients and existing clients. With strong relationships clients are maintained which is important in a very competitive market. From a media-relations perspective it can benefit the company's name recognition.

It is important to maintain a relationship with current customers through service appointments for the opportunity to sell them their next job, to learn about what challenges they may be facing and to further position your firm as their problem solver. E-marketing helps one stay in touch in a cost-effective manner.

WANT PROOF?

Not yet convinced about e-marketing capabilities? Jupiter Research projects that e-mail marketing spending will grow from $1.2 billion in 2007 to $2.1 billion in 2012. Spending on retention e-mail will more than double during that period and account for over half of total e-mail marketing spending in 2012. Acquisition e-mail marketing will grow somewhat more slowly, with most spending in that category going toward sponsorship, i.e., ad-supported e-newsletters). While this trend represents a shift from old media to new media, it in no way suggests tactics of the past are becoming extinct.

Traditional media will continue to play an important role in the local market. But it's essential to transition customers to new media before competitors do yet the ability to assemble large audiences in the local market will remain a principal advantage of traditional media.

Getting started in e-marketing can require an investment in software and training. The ongoing costs however are minimal. While some e-marketing is done without the print component many find a combined or multi-channel approach to be the most effective. Consider that you are likely to be well positioned to offer services your clients need, albeit with a new online service. You may already have the sales people, relationships and contacts needed that many other companies do not. A marriage of the two may catapult your business forward.

E-marketing can deliver a reduction in the costs of traditional marketing while providing the potential for a faster client/prospect response. It also offers an improved ability to measure and collect data, can cost-effectively open new markets and furnish increased interactivity and contact. Disadvantages include the absence of a personal approach or touch. It also increases your businesses' dependence on technology while opening you up to the greater competitive forces of the worldwide web. Customers obtained this way are usually more price sensitive as they have the ability to quote from competitors virtually anywhere and may be less loyal than traditional ones.

The most effective way to get prospects to open your e-mail is to make it informative the first time you've e-mailed them. In the "e-world," as in the sales world the first impression is critical. If you have a very informative offer, be sure it's worded right and use "a benefit-rich headline." Similar to direct mail, provide useful, original content and results should follow.

Be selective when purchasing an e-list. To manage the addresses and avoid "spam," reputable e-mail list brokers always send your e-mails for you. This helps them keep the list from falling into irresponsible hands. Similarly, do not send unsolicited e-mails. Instead, add a "sign- up" feature to your site to obtain recipients' permission before e-mailing them.

If you're not involved in it already e-marketing should be high on your priority list. This potentially helpful phenomenon is performance-based and presents low risk for those looking for the next big thing. The fact that it requires a low initial investment and relatively simple start-up training makes it even more attractive. Over time, marketers who strive to put the latest practices to work should be at the lead in driving the most traffic to their sites, resulting in a growing number of sales.

CHAPTER 8
IT ALL COMES DOWN TO INTEGRATED MARKETING

THE IMPORTANCE OF FLYING IN FORMATION

Every move you make says something about you and your firm. Whether you do it yourself or work with a pro, an **Integrated Marketing** platform should provide guidelines as to how your firm is portrayed.

What's integrated marketing? You've probably heard the phrase. If you haven't, you probably will the next time you meet with a marketing professional to discuss ways to grow your business. If you're not sure what integrated marketing is, don't feel embarrassed because chances are you're not alone.

Everyone's heard this phrase as well: Fly in formation. To succeed in integrated marketing that's what you must do. Every aspect of your company, from its logo to its letterhead, from its website and e-mail to its direct-mail package and trade show booth must reflect one, unified image. The bonus behind this is that when properly done, it sends a strong, unmistakable presence about you and your brand.

Consider some of the world's most famous logos such as the blue square of American Express, the golden arches of McDonald's or the white script on red panel that means Coca-Cola. These are world-recognized brands and for good reason. No matter where you are, once you see those logos you know you'll receive a certain level of quality and service. They represent certain standard levels that customers anywhere in the world can depend on. If you're disappointed, there's a formal complaint process where someone will look into your grievance and compensate you if warranted. Companies work hard and spend tirelessly to defend and grow their brands.

It's not enough to be satisfied with the status quo because everything around us has changed and will continue to do so. This is important when it comes to growing your business. It's not enough to use the latest and greatest in technology if you're still relying on your father's and grandfather's marketing methods.

Integrated marketing, according to the Marketing Power Dictionary, has come to mean a "holistic approach" to promote buying and selling in the digital economy. It means positioning your company as more than a service or product provider but rather as a brand that's to remain consistent, dependable and relevant. What's integrated is each of the many components that define your brand or your business's "unique personality." To fully utilize integrated marketing you need to invest in the full-court press that involves every aspect of your company's image, profile and mission statement. It's not enough to say things like: "The customer is always right," or "We under-promise and over-deliver."

The phrase "add value" has significance to this new generation of customers who will probably locate your company through Internet Search Engine Optimization (SEO) rather than through an ad or a friend's referral. Even if they do get a referral to you from a friend or colleague, most likely they'll check you out on the Internet before picking up the telephone. In the absence of a recommendation, they will probably "surf the web" in search of that "right promise." Geographic location will be a very small factor. If they locate you on the web they will then probably visit your website and attempt to learn what other customers may have experienced in a chat room before sending an e-mail asking for further information. Therefore, a good integrated marketing plan should include: e-mail marketing, web banner ads, a blog, podcasts and possibly Internet TV. Each of these should be designed to complement any traditional or "off-line marketing" methods, such as the traditional print, mail order, public relations and trade show efforts with each of them working together as a "virtual team" marching towards the goal line.

One of the often unexpected perks behind a successful integrated marketing campaign is that they are generally not prohibitively expensive. In fact, marketing technology can help the smaller company as much as the larger one. In this area technology truly levels the playing field between the individual or smaller partnership vs. the conglomerate.

TECHNOLOGY HELPS THE SMALLER FIRM AS MUCH AS IT HELPS THE LARGER ONE.

E-blast campaigns, coupled with social networking participation like LinkedIn, Fast Pitch, Konnects, Facebook, and more traditional methods such as Business Network International, Chamber of Commerce events, industry-specific events, etc., allow small firms to achieve greater results at a lower cost. E-blasts allow firms to keep in touch with current and potential clients on a regular basis, for less money than a traditional direct-mail campaign. Include case studies as you continue to educate prospects about specific services you provide, adding short testimonials from happy clients for instant credibility.

All e-marketing should be simple (see Chapter 7). They should be "easy to navigate, brief (under 200 words) and of course informative and attractively designed." Send 7-12 e-blasts per year following the above rules plus feature a promotion or special offer and mention any positive press coverage your firm may have received.

One obstacle to an effective integrated marketing campaign is that by using a variety of media, one runs the risk of overloading and potentially confusing and upsetting both staff and customers. This is why using the same images and messages across the marketing board is critical. Each component needs to help move the firm closer to achieving its goal and staff must understand this in order to use it to build the business. While each medium has different strengths and weaknesses, the goal remains to grow the firm. Staffers need to be taught not to fear or mistrust any new mediums or methods but to view them with an open mind. Some staff will buy into a new marketing program from the start, appreciating the fact that the firm has recognized a changing playing field and is taking new steps to thrive in it. Others will come on board once they see the results, which is why management needs to be steadfast and thorough once it decides to pursue an integrated marketing strategy.

Ultimately, integrated marketing is much more than the means to an end. In fact, it's not an end at all but a beginning of a new day for your company. Embrace it. Learn about it and thrive with it.

CHAPTER 9
TALK TO ME

CLIENT COMMUNICATION 101

While the rules of business are seemingly always changing, at the end of the day it's actually for each of us more about being in the client-satisfaction industry than anything else. Since each client brings a unique set of requirements to the relationship how does today's businessperson keep each one satisfied while growing the company in a steadily progressing industry where the ball is constantly in play?

Client communications lie at the heart and soul of each sales practice and can pay dividends in more ways than one. Clients usually appreciate the direct and active approach you may take to managing their expectations. This should be based on meaningful questions designed to take the relationship beyond price. In addition to strong client loyalty, the regular goal should be to earn business-building referrals and new projects.

While technology always promises to help us do more with less, there's no substitute for spending time with a client and in the process, make a better client out of a current one by building on the existing relationship. This can be more efficient than trying to cultivate business from a new prospect and entails more than taking a client to golf or dinner.

What do you say to a client when aiming to build a better relationship? Ask what keeps them up at night? What do they worry about? They'd rather being do what they do best than worrying about things like taxes, insurance, personnel, profit-and-loss statements, continuity planning, competition and marketing.

CAN YOU REMOVE CLIENT ANXIETY?

Thriving business people are able to "remove anxiety" from the murky equation that's become clients' lives. Look for cues to this phenomenon as the best ones make you aware that there's a question that needs to be answered somewhere in the prospect's life. Understandably, a person is more predictably ready to complain about their business future in a one-on-one meeting than in the presence of others. When you hear such cues respond by taking ample time to learn more about what underlies the frustration then offer your services which may alleviate their situation, thus removing the anxiety.

Psychologists teach us that, fundamentally, human behavior is driven by two basic forces: the desire to avoid pain and the desire to gain pleasure. Of those two, the more powerful is the desire to avoid pain. Armed with this knowledge, once you realize a prospect's pain/anxiety level and can equate working with you to the reduction or removal of that pain, you're more likely to gain a client.

One of the keys to steady success is to not overwhelm the client with too much information or too many ideas at once. Often as you work with a client, you will hear other things that are issues for them, like perhaps they need more time and have problems making future plans. Consider this as an opportunity to assist. You can also learn a lot by working with the client in their environment, i.e., home/office. In their own environment, prospects are more relaxed. This means you may be able to see the kinds of situations in front of them. Keep mind of the old saying: Don't spill your popcorn in the lobby. This means give your client or prospect a chance to tell you what they need and want. Don't first tell them everything about you and your company.

Another key question: What was the original need for getting together? This sounds basic but can often get lost. Then ask how their situation may have changed or how they anticipate it changing. Is a new product on the way? When might they like to retire? It's critical to keep questions simple and follow an educational approach when trying to move from "No" to "Yes." While there are numerous ways to address client problems, by giving them a chance to tell you what they need and want and by being thoughtful and open minded in your approach, solutions as well as sales should follow.

Frequently the obvious items of importance are commonly uncovered in basic client-information questionnaires but the more subtle clues, the ones that can lead to deeper, longer lasting relationships and true problem solving are often revealed in conversations. Finding ways to spend more time with clients is therefore critical to providing solutions that can grow business.

If a new client is heard to say something like: "I feel so awful that I haven't done anything about this," that statement can be translated as a pain that you may be able to relieve. Such language is most likely to come out in a one-on-one meeting. When you hear it, repeat the emotional language and inquire further, take the time to learn more about what underlies the statement and then offer your services in that context: "I hear you saying that you're frustrated. Can I show you a way so that you may feel confident that your future will evolve in the way you've imagined?"

Or: "I've heard you mention several areas you can improve by working with us. Would you like to see how we can help today?"

Business today is more relationship driven as factors like the Internet have leveled the pricing-playing field in nearly every industry. Not only can it pay to explain to clients the various ways in which you can save money, many now expect this type of treatment from their sales representatives. It's no longer a price-driven business. Service is key.

And then the issue remains, if your clients aren't getting the service and support they're expecting from you, someone else, probably a more intense marketer, will offer it and probably take your customer. It hurts to lose a client but when something like this occurs, all you can do is backpedal and try to win back your now former client. Chances are you'll be operating from a position of weakness since they'll want to know why you didn't treat them right in the first place.

THE WELCOME EDUCATOR

You usually do not have to create a need -- one is always somewhere. The needs will generally expose themselves over the course of conversation and the solutions then become logical conclusions. Getting in front of the prospects is usually the challenge. What kind of educational material can you furnish to make prospects want to meet with you or respond to your ad or direct mail piece? Points about technological advantages offered by your office or skills provided by key staff members can be great conversation starters which can be supplemented with illustrations and examples of the work they've produced. A special offer such as no-charge initial consultation can also help. The aim is to whet the client's appetite to do business with you. Build rapport because none of us likes to be "sold."

Education and conversation build relationships which can build business. You increase your credibility when beginning meetings with data that is valuable to the prospect. Start each meeting by teaching your prospect something new or by distributing data that shows you're prepared.

The answer to running a more efficient, solutions-based practice lies with our willingness to commit to an ongoing communications strategy. While this is easier said than done, very likely the businessperson who spends more time with clients to better understand them is the one who can offer on-target solutions to help fill their needs and win their loyalty.

CHAPTER 10
WHAT ABOUT ETHICS?

IF NOT NOW, WHEN?

Business people periodically take time from their routine, distance themselves from the day-to-day operations and try to plan for their futures. The close of one year and the start of the next are frequently good times to reflect on what took place during the past 12 months and set the stage for better things to come. How to grow your business or meet bigger sales goals are common themes along with losing weight and spending more time with the family. But amid all the fantasies about getting faster, stronger and bigger do we ever stop to think about being more ethical?

While nearly each of us pays lip service to the importance of business ethics, numerous headlines prove that the practice is not a reality for many whether you're trading commodities on Wall St. or selling hamburgers on Main St. Further still, can you thrive as a business if you're taking advantage of your neighbor? Hurting the environment? Cheating a supplier, your insurer or the government?

Is there a relationship between ethics and business success or is "business ethics" a contradiction in terms? Many feel the corporate world is responsible for some of the biggest problems to beset mankind. As business people we are an extension and representation of this. Do we even need an official ethics policy or is our awareness to "do the right thing" for our clients adequate? Can a business driven by integrity and earnest leadership practices actually have an advantage over its competitors? Will it outperform in areas like employee turnover, teamwork, client retention and overall business reputation?

Tackling business ethics is an area too wide to be sufficiently addressed here. A simple web search will produce endless "experts" on the topic. Similarly, contemplation of the numerous issues each of us confronts puts us face-to-face with choices that have ethical implications on a daily basis. Consider the following:

Do my clients know all the fees I'm charging them?

Do my clients understand agreements they may be signing?

Which supplier do I choose, the one that sends me on vacations or the one with lesser fees or better products?

Should I do business with those exhibiting questionable behavior?

Have I done my due diligence?

Is my marketing completely truthful?

Do I disparage competitors?

Who do I turn to for guidance?

Each of these questions generates more reflection, such as: How do these actions impact how I am perceived by my clients? By my community? By my fellow business people? And in turn, how does this affect my business? And the big one: What if I get caught?

While some attempts at moral guidance have periodically (and ironically) come from Washington, a code of ethics should set out ideals for ethical conduct based on fundamental principles of openness, integrity, honesty and trust. A good code of ethics should effectively convey to everyone with whom you come in contact the value you place on ethical conduct and should be communicated to your employees.

But do we really need formal ethics and conduct requirements? Shouldn't behaving ethically be a part of our daily practice no matter which profession we choose?

WHAT TO DO

When providing information about your company, it is a good practice to include its ethical principles, credo or code on your website, in your brochures and in any other marketing-communications materials. You may have a corporate social-responsibility report. Do you help others through your business, i.e. are you aligned with a charity in a meaningful way? These are good signs that your company is serious about workplace ethics.

Some businesses actually make ethics a cornerstone in their marketing by outwardly positioning themselves as forthright and trustworthy in each of their business communications.

Just as our economy was recovering from the post-Enron world, it had a relapse thanks to a string of Wall St., real estate and banking failures and scandals. This begs one to ask: is there a ROI (Return on Integrity) with an organization that emphasizes fair business principles. Can you successfully operate on principles of fairness? Will doing the right thing for your clients actually help your business succeed?

We'd like to say "yes" and there are plenty of business examples to prove this. But are these the rule or the exception? Ethics are not a glamorous part of business. We'd rather hear stories of business people climbing back from ruin and regaining corporate stature or news of mergers and acquisitions than of someone methodically trying to do the right thing each day simply because it's the right thing to do.

While many in numerous industries have rightly been taken to task for misconduct, take solace in the fact that most of us have probably helped a great deal of people in more ways than we can remember.

If you've never given the idea of incorporating ethics into your business than you can start by asking the question: how would my business thrive if I made a conscious decision to formally include ethical conduct goals and standards into our structure? Could we gain by helping others? Where will the time and other resources come from to help us achieve this objective? Should we promote this aspect of our business or should we keep our good deeds to ourselves?

Think about what the consequences may be if you do not do such things. We live in a world where communication is increasingly plentiful and rapid. Any employee or business associate can enter a number of websites and post disparaging information about your company or its key leaders should either behave in a socially irresponsible manner. A simple Google search can draw up numerous listings of nearly any company. Wouldn't you want as many of them as possible to be positive ones? A healthy and practical ethics code can make employees, even unhappy ones, reluctant to take disparaging steps or speak harshly about you and your company.

Your business does not operate in a vacuum or exist on an island. It interacts with its clients, suppliers, neighbors and environment on a regular basis. Can you as a business person fulfill an obligation to society to help the greater good and still grow profits?

You absolutely can and you absolutely should do so now.

www.ingramcontent.com/pod-product-compliance
Lightning Source LLC
Chambersburg PA
CBHW081230170526
45165CB00009B/3020